The Parents Guide to Autism

Anne Carol Sharples

ISBN: 978-1-77277-023-0

PUBLISHED BY:
10-10-10 PUBLISHING
MARKHAM, ON
CANADA

Contents

A heartfelt thank you to Lori Ravensborg, Graham, Connor and Zoe Schofield for sharing their story. It is through stories that we connect emotionally, exchange information and learn lessons.

Lori, your honesty and down to earth approach when sharing the struggles you face as a parent, captures the heart of all who read your words. The courage, patience, strength and love you demonstrate every day for your children is admirable. Both Zoe and Connor are blessed to have you as their mom.

Connor, thank you for coining the phrase "goosebumps on steroids" to describe the anxiety you sometimes feel. Your description and the ease with which you explained things to me is of profound value to so many.

Zoe, your depth of insight and level of awareness is extraordinary. Interviewing you and seeing your creative and inquisitive nature blossom is a rare find. Thank you for openly sharing what life is like for you.

Acknowledgements

It is with much love and respect that this book is dedicated to the individuals on the autism spectrum, their families and caregivers.

To the many teachers and support staff I work with daily. Your commitment to serving individuals on the autism spectrum is inspirational.

To Raymond Aaron, whose encouragement ignited the spark within me. Without you, this book would not exist.

To Doctor Stuart Shanker for his expertise, dedication and care for each child and family he works with. Your contribution to the educational communities and teachers is invaluable.

To my Dad, for his countless hours of editing and reviewing of this book, at the drop of a hat. He even edited a draft while vacationing down south. Your encouragement and support is limitless; as is my love for you.

To my greatest gifts; my sons James and Matthew. You are my greatest teachers.

Foreword
by Dr. Stuart Shanker

All children have the same need: to feel safe and secure. And all children have the same vulnerability: they are easily frightened by a world they don't yet understand; by loud noises and flashing lights; adults who tower over them; animals or for that matter insects that come rushing up; other children who make incomprehensible demands on them; a body that refuses to do what they want from it, or sends its own incomprehensible and often painful messages.

This latent fearfulness that can easily grip all children starts incredibly early: from the very moment, in fact, when the newborn is exposed to a world, inner as well as outer, that pushes her ability to stay calm beyond its limits. It is only through the soothing ministrations of their caregiver that a "kindled alarm" can be turned off. But for a significant number of babies – a number that seems to be growing every year – this sensory assault is more than even the Interbrain can contend with.

The Interbrain is a "wireless" right-brain to right-brain hookup that enables a caregiver to read and respond to her baby's need for up- or down-regulating. But for a child with autism, sounds and sights and smells and touches may not just be aversive: they can be over-powering. When that happens, the baby shuts down and shuts out her caregiver as a means of self-protection. But such actions not only interfere with the fine-tuned operations of the Interbrain: they obstruct the very interactive experiences that are needed in order to develop the capacity to deal with the sensory/social world that the child finds so overwhelming.

This is what happens to so many of the children born with autism: because of their neurogenetic deficits, they adopt defensive behaviours that block the very nurturing experiences that every child needs in order to learn language; develop emotionally; learn how to mindread; learn how to read and write; build meaningful relationships with others; find a passion; nurture their imagination; discover, not just a meaningful life, but a life full of meaning.

We now have so much research – more than we could ever hope to summarize – telling us that education is absolutely pivotal to achieving these developmental goals. Every parent wants for their child to experience the joys and the untold benefits of education: social and personal as well as academic and professional. Granted, going to school can be frightening for any young child; but for a child with autism, a child who is already primed to go into fight-or-flight at the slightest provocation, it can be more than they can bear.

Yet there are so many things that we can do to ease the child's entry into schooling, and indeed, so many things we can do to ease the anguish of their parents during this process. What every child with autism, and every parent of a child with autism most needs from all of us is understanding. *The Parents Guide to Autism* is filled with all sorts of very practical suggestions to help children with autism, and their parents, cope with the many stresses involved in schooling, and indeed, positively thrive there. But first and foremost comes understanding.

Anne Carol Sharples sets out in this book to "Create a world of informed and educated individuals who are inclusive rather than fearful." It is an invaluable book for parents with children on the autism spectrum. It is an invaluable book for all of us. In fact, I wondered when I put it down whether it might have been better titled: *A Parent's Guide to Children.*

Dr. Stuart Shanker

Founder and Chief Executive Officer, The MEHRIT Centre

Dr. Stuart Shanker is a Distinguished Research Professor of Philosophy and Psychology at York University and the CEO of the MEHRIT Centre, Ltd. (www.self-reg.ca). One of his many books, "Calm, Alert and Learning: Classroom Strategies for Self-Regulation (2012)", is the top selling educational publication ever in Canada. His new book "Self-Reg: How to help your child (and you) break the stress-cycle and successfully engage with life" will be published June 2016.

Over the past decade, Stuart has served as an advisor on early child development to government organizations across Canada and the US, and in countries around the world. He served as the 2012 Thinker in Residence for Western Australia. In Canada, he is assisting in Kindergarten to grade 12 Self-Reg initiatives in school jurisdictions across the country. Stuart cares deeply about the health and well-being of children and families, and what is every bit as important to him, is the health and well-being of teachers. He commits considerable time to bringing the research and science of Self-Reg to early childhood educators, teachers, educational leaders, health practitioners and communities through presentations, online courses, webinars, publications, social media and most recently a blog entitled, "The Self-Reg View".

Chapter 1

The Diagnosis of Autism

Autism is one of the fastest growing developmental disorders in Canada and the United States. Over the past ten years, the number of diagnoses has almost doubled. The million dollar question is why? This is an issue that is highly debated. Are we more aware of what to look for as parents? Are physicians better at diagnosing? Is it advanced paternal age? Genetics? Maternal exposure to certain agents? As much as we have learned, there is so much that we don't know. But the purpose of this book is not to write about the cause of autism. The purpose is to guide parents. Let's start by defining what autism is.

Autism is a broad spectrum and not one single condition. A spectrum that ranges from John who is a 15 year old with a diagnosis of autism. John is non-verbal and communicates through a device. He points to pictures on his iPad to indicate his wants and needs. John is sensitive to the sound of an airplane and lawnmowers and appears to hear them way before anyone around him can. Strong perfumes and soaps make him want to gag. When upset, John engages in self-injurious behaviors. He will bang his head on a wall or desk and wears a helmet to protect his head from injury. John attends a special class outside of his local school neighborhood. There are eight students in his class.

That same diagnosis of autism also applies to Mark who is 15 years old. Mark is in grade ten and has the highest average in his class. He excels academically but Mark has great difficulty navigating the social world. He appears unaware of the social conventions and says that he is often at a loss for words when in social situations. Mark doesn't know what to say or do when he is with his peers. He has difficulty understanding the perspectives and viewpoints of others. The other day, Mark was talking to his locker partner about his favorite movie and did not tune into his locker partner's yawns and wandering eyes indicating a lack of interest.

Both John and Mark have the same diagnosis, and both present very differently. Autism is a broad spectrum.

Although each individual on the autism spectrum presents differently, some common characteristics are inflexibility and rigidity, sensory issues, emotional regulation and communication challenges. An individual on the autism spectrum may be unable to speak. Another may have very high verbal skills and abilities. Communication deficits, inability to self-regulate and sensory integration issues are all characteristics that an individual on the autism spectrum may experience. Yet, no two individuals experience this spectrum in the same way.

What we do know is that early diagnosis is critical. There are many tools and a lot more information out there indicating red flags for parents. If you are concerned about something, a visit to a physician is recommended. Be prepared for the appointment, as this can be an overwhelming time. Write a list indicating what concerns you have, and prepare a series of questions you would like answered. Keep the paper handy so that you can refer to it whenever a thought or question pops up. Take video. We have the technology at our fingertips with cell phones today. Providing a video of your child interacting, requesting something or engaging in play would also be helpful to a physician. Bring a friend or family member with you for support. Don't hesitate to ask your physician how familiar he or she is with autism spectrum disorder and whether or not he or she has worked directly with individuals on the autism spectrum. Ask them how familiar they are with Dr. Ami Klin and Dr. Warren Jones' work on eye tracking and whether or not they use this to screen infants with autism spectrum disorder. If you are uncomfortable with what you are hearing, or you have doubts, get a second opinion, or a third. Ask questions; share your concerns about things.

Receiving a diagnosis can be devastating, and shock and grief are normal reactions. It most certainly isn't what was expected. Being told that your child cannot do things or your child will struggle are things parents do not want to hear. It can be a time when parents experience extreme loneliness, sadness, anger or denial, until acceptance is finally reached.

Lori, a mother of a son they classified as Asperger's, shares her experience when her son received a diagnosis at the age of eight.

"I am incredibly thankful for the diagnosis because our six year journey started to make sense. At the age of five Connor was diagnosed with sensory integration. Walking barefoot on the grass or sand was painful for him. He would spit out new food, and wearing jeans would hurt him. As he began school in the primary grades, we began to notice more issues revolving around his peers and social communication, (eg. personal space, rigid and reactive responses) which led us back to the drawing board of deeper assessment ....That's when Connor was diagnosed with Asperger Syndrome. Prior to the diagnosis, when I experienced days of frustration I could not attribute them to anything but take the blame myself; it must be miscalculations in my own parenting, I thought. So, I feel a certain relief and I can wander through the process of the diagnosis and my son being under the umbrella. I feel like I can legitimize our experience somehow and I can feel better about finding strategies. I don't have to take as much of the self-judgment and take as much in of the other judgment that comes in my direction."

Once a diagnosis is made, and as a parent you have come to terms with it, your new journey begins. Learning about autism from reliable sources, observing your child; recognizing their strengths and needs and advocating for them is your new role. As a parent, you become your child's voice. The diagnosis is a part of your child, it is not all of your child. Your child is the blue-eyed redhead who comes running to the door when you arrive home and leaps into your arms. Your child is the child who squeals in delight when he sees Julia, a muppet with autism on Sesame Street. Being your child's voice means speaking up when out in the community, in school, and out in the world.

Unfortunately, there are far too many unpleasant experiences to account for, with people who say hurtful, insensitive things. Things like: Can't you control your kid? You are a lousy parent, or What's wrong with your kid? As difficult as it may be in the moment, the point here is not to surround yourself in a downward spiral of negativity, but rather to lift yourself up and educate someone. Society has its stereotypes and we as parents may find ourselves in a situation where we are ostracized. Our child may be ostracized. We may be told that our child is too difficult to handle on a play date. Or we may be asked questions like, Why does your child walk like that? Why does your child look like that? Your child may experience bullying.

Lori gives an example of this.

"You will hear people talk about when my kid was two or three and we were in the supermarket and he had a meltdown and freaked out, and I had to leave my cart of groceries at the checkout. People understand when the child is a toddler, but people don't understand when the child is a ten year old."

By being our child's voice we can begin a movement; spark change, build awareness and ultimately inclusivity. As parents we can round up supporters, build networks in schools, communities, cities and countries. Let's create a world of informed and educated individuals who are inclusive rather than fearful.

We also need to teach our children how to advocate for themselves as one day they will be adults, and we as parents will not always be there for them. Teach them to speak up in whatever way they can. If they want something, teach them to say and act on it. Having your child ask for something or get something on their own, and not rushing in as a parent to the rescue, is sometimes tough but absolutely necessary to build independence and advocacy skills. Providing praise and positive feedback will encourage your child to continue on the road of self-advocacy.

Teaching our children to self-advocate is the stepping stone to teaching independence and being a contributing members of society. We all have dreams for our children and want them to be able to be a part of something. Employment is an opportunity to contribute. It is an opportunity to figure out where we fit in and a place where we can share our gifts and talents. Some individuals on the spectrum are talented artistically and can share their gift with the world, doing what they love. This makes it easier to contribute and create. But what if your child doesn't have a particular skill or talent that is so prevalent? This is where building on your child's interests fits in. Perhaps he or she has a special interest in vacuum cleaners, or sport statistics; maybe your child likes reading diagrams and putting furniture together. Regardless of what it is, as a parent, we need to support it. The story of the father who had a child who loved to shred paper comes to mind when thinking about special interests. This love for shredding paper has now been built into a business. Whether it means knocking on doors of businesses that cater to your child's special interest or your child starting his or her own business, we need to change the statistics.

Tens of thousands of individuals with autism are looking for work in Canada and around the world. Many individuals on the spectrum are rejected by the labor market, deemed unemployable. Some may not even get past the front door because of the interview process. Sensory issues and deficits in social skills are often barriers that employers cannot see past. But they are barriers that, when worked through, can enable an individual on the autism spectrum to be a productive contributing member of society. Often we see a very capable individual on the autism spectrum collecting grocery carts when they have so much more to offer, and if given a chance would. This is where schools, communities and businesses need to work together to support this tsunami of individuals on the autism spectrum heading towards employment. Autism is on the rise. Let's change the number of individuals at home beyond the age of 21, who are currently isolated from society.

Chapter 2

It's All About Relationships

So, your child is beginning school. You have registered, provided the school with all the necessary paperwork but are feeling completely overwhelmed with worry. What happens next? These thoughts and feeling are not uncommon. Navigating the school system can sometimes feel like swimming upstream.

A parent's anguish

My story probably differs very little from a parent of a special needs child who is mainstreamed as they enter school for the very first time. My daughter is three, she turns four in November and it is her very first time in school.

I am overwhelmed with the class size; twenty-five four year olds. A handful of them have needs like my daughter. How can the teacher manage? How can I be reassured that my daughter is receiving the best care possible? I have so many questions and I feel that the school is leaving them unanswered.

I feel frustrated, helpless and alone. My daughter is not toilet trained, minimally verbal and I often wonder, how will they manage?

If there were one thing I would want every teacher, support staff and administrator to know, it would be that I am not trying to be difficult. My daughter is my number one priority and I will do whatever is necessary to ensure that she receives the care and support she needs. I am her voice, her advocate, her mother.

Let's take it from the beginning. Your child turns four this year and you have just registered him at the local school. What's next? There are many things that can be done in preparation for the big transition. Begin by introducing yourself. Forging a relationship with the people who will now be an extension of you as a parent is important. Your child will spend a significant portion of their day in school. Relationship building, showing support and working together can alleviate a lot of stress and worry. Begin building a portfolio of your child; their strengths, likes and dislikes. This can be shared with the teacher at the beginning of school. Portfolios are most helpful, as they provide a snapshot and allow the teacher to read your child very quickly. The portfolio is representative of all of the correct tools in the toolbox. Figuring out a child's likes and dislikes can take a long time and by equipping the teacher with the right set of tools from the start, we are all way ahead of the game.

Once school begins, relationship building with teacher and support staff begins. Share the portfolio, and anything else that would help the teacher in working with your child. Find out which mode of communication the teacher prefers and use it. Some prefer email, others a handwritten note and others a phone call.

If there is a question or concern, speak with the teacher first. Building relationship involves trust and open lines of communication. No one likes it when you go above their heads and ask a principal about something that could have been resolved and discussed with the teacher. Go to the source first.

If feasible, approach the principal to offer your assistance with activities that are going on within the school. Perhaps there is a fundraising activity or a food drive that the school is involved in that you could assist with. This is an opportunity to establish your own credibility, keep your agreements, follow through with your promises and time commitments, complete tasks and demonstrate your own integrity. Providing a helping hand is very much appreciated. It also allows the administration and staff in the school to see you taking the lead and working collaboratively for the same cause. If volunteering doesn't render to your schedule, join the parent committee in the school. Being an active member and participant in the school community demonstrates your level of commitment and it keeps you informed.

Always attend meetings. Sometimes, there may be a box on a form coming home that indicates that you give permission to proceed without the parent/guardian being present. Do not check this off, regardless of what message is conveyed. Always attend, be on time, listen attentively and avoid being adversarial. Be present for events at school as well. If there is a bake sale, participate in whatever way is possible for you. Be involved.

If your child is overtired the first few weeks of school, stick to routines. Ensure that he eats and sleeps as well as possible and communicate this with the teacher. He won't be the only one. Beginning a new routine, meeting new staff, starting a new experience, attending school for the very first time requires an adjustment. Many teachers have a communication booklet that goes home daily. There is a space provided for home and a space provided for school. Mentioning how your child's evening went, what activities he was involved in, how he slept, and whether or not he ate breakfast before school are all key components to how his day will go. They are very helpful and explain many things. A sample of a communication booklet between home and school can be downloaded on my website. Visit www.annecarolsharples.com.

Remember that the common goal here is to provide your child with the best possible learning experience. Communicating with the teacher, sharing information and things that are going on at home that may affect your child such as a move, a job loss, a new sibling, a visiting relative, sharing a bedroom are helpful tidbits of information that demonstrate open communication and building of relationship. While visiting many schools, the common thread that I have noticed is that there is always a renewed sense of trust following parent-teacher interviews. Teachers feel great when they have connected with parents, discussed their concerns and are building a relationship with their partners in education – you.

So, you have forged a relationship with the people who spend a great deal of time with your child each and every day. Now it is time to build relationships within your own neighborhood and community. Having a strong, supportive network of peers in and out of class is so important. Look for children the same age and who live nearby. Perhaps you have noticed them in the playground, at drop off and pick up time. Maybe they wait at the bus stop. There could be names your child mentions to you. Approach and begin building the relationship with the parent or caregiver. Arranging a play date at the local park is a great way to start. It is an opportunity to observe how well the children play together, if they share common interests, if they are empathetic, compassionate and supportive of your child. It is amazing what you can learn through observation. And while the children play, the adults can also get to know each other. People are curious and may want to know why your child may not respond to his name all the time, or may not make eye contact. This is the perfect time to discuss autism and how it is a part of him. Educating, discussing and sharing information is a way to build a more inclusive world and a way to erase stereotypical attitudes.

There are many times, as a parent of a child on the autism spectrum, that we may find ourselves in an awkward moment. Perhaps your child is having a meltdown in a shopping mall because the Lego set he has wanted is sold out. Maybe he has asked why the man next to him is so fat. Regardless of the scenario, as a parent we have all experienced the feeling of wanting to disappear.

Lori, a mother of a son they classified as Asperger's describes how she feels in situations where her son is experiencing a high level of stress and anxiety.

A lot of effort is made, trying to avoid a lot of high anxiety situations and meltdown situations so you don't have to deal with those situations – but when you do have to deal with them and there is no escape, you feel judged. It is very easy for people to judge you, as a parent or as a kid. It is a lack of knowledge. When I find myself in this predicament, sometimes I educate, sometimes I walk away, sometimes I get angry, sometimes I take it out on those closest to me.

When people judge a situation or react in a certain way, they lack knowledge. Behavior that does not fit into the mold society has expected stands out. It is our responsibility as parents and educators to educate everyone about autism. Starting a parent group in your school community, taking a stand, and supporting each other are ways to begin the process. Public libraries and church halls provide a space where this can be done. Finding people within your circle to speak about autism is a simple and effective way to educate people.

Your child starting school is a rite of passage. It can be an overwhelming feeling as a parent to hand over the reins to people you don't know. That is why developing and continually building a relationship with your child's teacher, support staff and principal is critical. Being coordinated, aligning all of the vectors and having your child's development at the center is what is required in order for him to blossom and reach his potential; it is our duty as parents, educators and members of the community.

Chapter 3

How We Learn and The People That Help Us

When we want to teach our children something, we need to look at where they are and what they understand. To start teaching them something that is above their head would leave them with many gaps, and missing bits of information. Think of teaching someone to multiply before they know how to add. Since multiplying involves adding, it would seem silly to even think that. When thinking about the natural sequence of events, try to envision how a baby learns to roll over. Initially he will begin lifting his head while on his tummy. This progresses to arching his back and lifting his shoulders and head. The position then is reminiscent of the yoga pose called cobra. From there he graduates to tensing his core and back muscles, gaining momentum and flipping onto his side and finally his back. All of these are the steps required to turn over. Think about learning to ride a bike and the sequence of steps required in order to master that skill. When we have the correct gradient, aka instructional level, we are starting at a good place.

When we want to teach something, we want to have the information and things needed to demonstrate the concept. If we want to learn about computers, it would be very helpful to have a computer in front of us. The same thing goes for cars. If learning how to change a tire, reading about it would not be as effective as actually doing it. Having the concrete object in front of us is an effective way of demonstrating how to do something. It allows us to learn visually, and by doing. Let's try learning how to play an instrument. Can you imagine what it would be like to learn how to play a musical instrument, say the piano, on a paper keyboard? Now a paper keyboard is better than no keyboard, but having the instrument in front of us is a far more powerful tool.

The third thing that ensures we are learning is the understanding of words. When we come across a word we do not know or understand, our learning stops. Here is an example. "Fashion has changed dramatically over the decades but one of the things I am most fond of is the winklepicker of the fifties." Now, having read the sentence, the likelihood is you understood everything until you read the word "winklepicker," and now, perhaps, you are a little lost. If I explained to you that the word "winklepicker" describes a shoe or boot style that had a pointed toe and was popular in the fifties, you would understand the sentence in its entirety. Let's try another exercise. On a blank sheet of paper, draw a large rectangle in the center of the page. Inside the rectangle, draw a chair, television, lamp, end table, and a causeuse. Add a bookshelf and a table lamp on the end table. Now, did you stop at causeuse? Did you skip over that instruction and continue? Were you confused? If I told you that the word causeuse meant a sofa built for two people, you would be able to continue the exercise with ease.

Receiving instructions at the appropriate level, having a visual representation, concrete object or the real thing, and understanding and knowing the meaning of words are critical components in learning.

As a parent we are our child's first teacher. As he grows, his world expands beyond home as does the network of people in his circle. He begins school and other players enter the scene. The role of teacher is to recognize where your child is and what he needs to learn to get to the next step. Each child in the class is at a different level. The skill and craft of a teacher is to reach each and every one of the children there, despite their levels, knowledge base and abilities. This is called differentiated instruction. The role of the teacher is to program for individual students. A teacher plans, set goals, and provides the tools necessary for this to be executed. Yet to a child, a teacher is so much more than this. If it is the child's first experience in school, a teacher is an extension of home life, a first contact outside of a familiar place like home. As your child grows, a teacher is a role model, a mentor, one who is interested in your child and his successes, as well as areas where he needs to grow.

Sometimes, there may be a support staff, otherwise known as a paraprofessional, that works in your child's classroom. Perhaps they spend part of the day with your child providing additional support in an area where he needs it. A paraprofessional works under the direction of the teacher, and the supervision of an administrator. As a paraprofessional, the delivery of service is their primary role. All programming and planning needs to come from the teacher. Goal setting, recording of progress, determining learning materials needed for a student are all the responsibility of the teacher. A paraprofessional's responsibility is to assist the student with learning the material by implementing the techniques, strategies and appropriate language discussed or modelled. Gathering and sharing relevant information with the teacher is another responsibility of the paraprofessional. It is not the paraprofessional's role to make day to day decisions about your child, nor is it helpful for your child to spend a substantial part of his day in the company of the paraprofessional and miss out on meaningful experiences and opportunities to engage with his peers during recess and lunch. There is something wrong with this picture: a paraprofessional deciding when your child is in and out of the class and not the teacher, a paraprofessional providing programming for your child and not the teacher. In addition to the individual roles, there are also shared responsibilities that the teacher and paraprofessional have. Things such as discussing plans, reviewing resources, discussing progress and the child's learning profile, discussing successful practices and techniques, strategies and effective language. As a parent and advocate for your child, it is important to be aware of these roles and responsibilities.

Often times, boundaries get blurred when it comes to roles and responsibilities of teachers and paraprofessionals. Education around this is needed. This can begin in the Faculties of Education. It is important to teach teachers about their partners in education; the paraprofessionals and the role they play in education. Clearly, our education system and our classrooms have changed over the past few decades, and with this we all need to change. When there is no education there is a lack of knowledge that exists amongst the staff. Teachers learning to navigate through the different roles and responsibilities of the paraprofessionals, without being taught about this, is like driving without a destination in mind. There needs to be education and clear boundaries established on the different roles and how they play out in the classroom. A nurturing, collaborative environment and rapport between paraprofessionals and teachers needs to be established. This is where administration can step in at the beginning of each school year and review the roles and responsibilities and the expectations of teachers and paraprofessionals. This can avoid situations where a paraprofessional assumes the role of "teacher". Sometimes, teachers may feel that they lack the knowledge to teach students with special needs but appear to be quite willing to hand over the reins to a paraprofessional, falsely assuming that they know what to do. When a teacher hears they are receiving support for a student with a disability, the reaction is often one of relief that there is an extra set of hands to support and teach the special needs students in the class. But rather than focus on the tree, focus on the forest. How is this supporting our students? How is handing over the reins assisting? How is doing this promoting inclusivity within the classroom? Or, are we encouraging stigma? Although all people involved in education can benefit from additional courses and training in specialized areas, a student with special needs can benefit from the existing skills that teachers possess. The principles of teaching do not change just because a student has a label. Establishing roles and responsibilities can deter teachers from relinquishing the instruction of the student with special needs to the paraprofessional. Assuming that all paraprofessionals have the training to work with a variety of students is often the wrong assumption. This is not to say that a paraprofessional lacks the education, but, for the most part, they are often less qualified than the classroom teachers are when it comes to education and experience.

As a parent, it is important to be a keen observer and be aware of what is going on in your child's classroom. Ask questions, be involved and aware. A paraprofessional is there to empower and encourage your child, and then step back and allow your child to do things on his or her own. This is a critical component; the independence piece. At all costs we as parents and educators do not want to see the overdependence some students have on paraprofessionals. Some students develop a learned helplessness, knowing that the paraprofessional will come to the rescue so there is no need to forge forward. Some students feel the stigma because of the extra support they receive, or they are self-conscious and concerned about how they are viewed by others because they are shadowed constantly. This is where we need to assess, and ask, is your child truly benefiting from the additional support?

When parents, teachers and paraprofessionals are in synch, goals and outcomes are discussed and fading of support is carefully planned. Well-designed plans and programs with clearly established roles and team partnerships are extremely valuable in the education of our students.

Every case is unique, just as every child, and their learning and communication styles are unique. But at the end of the day, as educators and parents we want our students and children to be as successful and independent as possible. Just like a business needs a business plan, our children need careful planning which must include plans for inclusive involvement, fading of supports and ways to forge independence. By planning, collaborating, and working together as a team with clearly defined responsibilities and boundaries our students with special needs can have the best of both worlds. Extra support in areas of need and independence.

Chapter 4

Taking a Closer Look

Parenting can sometimes leave us feeling frazzled. Running errands, working, preparing meals, helping with homework and spending quality time with our children can be exhausting. Compound this with a child who is upset, unable to communicate what is bothering him, or a child who is struggling socially in school and you have a recipe for meltdown. It could be a battle at the checkout of the grocery store or a tantrum in the middle of the dry cleaners. It may appear to come out of nowhere and for no apparent reason, but it happens. And you don't know why. Self-doubt sets in. You start to second-guess yourself. Questions such as now what do I do? And thoughts, often negative ones, enter your mind as you begin to question your own ability to parent. Wouldn't it be nice if there was a manual to turn to that would have all of the answers?

Cristina would spend hours at the kitchen table completing her math homework. The fact that free time followed the completion of homework did not shorten the process, nor did it alleviate the duration of the meltdowns. Cristina's parents were at a loss and didn't know what to do. They began exploring different parenting websites and online support groups. It wasn't until they came across an article about data collection and the importance of it that they decided to take a closer look at Cristina and what was happening.

Why collect data? We collect data to get information. Data collection enables us to report on and assess how our stocks are performing, how our company business is doing, what the housing market is like and, yes, to see how our child is doing. Teachers do this with students all of the time. Our own performance at work is evaluated and compared to previous year performances. Data collection is a way to gather and measure information. It is a way to take a closer look, to evaluate and to change things when needed.

Data collection looks at things in a systematic fashion and enables us to come up with outcomes. It does not rely on bias or opinion, but rather gives us an accurate picture of what we are looking at. Pretend you are an actor, and you have tried out for a part in an upcoming Broadway hit musical. You are evaluated by a panel of twenty individuals. The feedback is positive, with the exception of one comment. At the end of the day, which do you reflect on? Is it the nineteen positive comments or the one negative comment? The ratio of positive to negative is 19:1. In all likelihood, you focus on the negative comment; even though you had 19 positive comments. Unlike opinions or emotions, data is an accurate measure, and it is necessary in order to monitor and evaluate progress.

There are many ways to collect data. A simple way, is one we are all familiar with, we see it on television and at a sports event. This is count data. It is a tally of the number of times the hockey puck enters the net, or it could be the amount of correct answers a student has on a math fact sheet.

We can collect data on the length of time it takes to complete a task from day to day. This is called duration. If homework is a daily task your child has, you may want to collect the data for a week to obtain an average amount of time it takes to complete it. For a free sample of a duration data collection visit my website at www.annecarolsharples.com.

Analyzing your child's behavior can help you understand what is going on. In Cristina's case, the form of data collection her parents decided to use is called an ABC Chart. This is a form that looks at the behavior as well as what happened before and after. The A stands for the antecedent. This is what happened immediately before the behavior. Was your child asked to do something, was there an unexpected change in scheduling, did the smoke detector go off making a loud sound? There are also other things to consider that may not be evident. Things such as was your child tired, hungry, upset about something that happened at school? The B stands for the behavior and it is a description of factual information. What happened? What did you see? The C stands for Consequence, and this is what happened immediately following the behavior. This could be a change in environment, a reaction from others, attention given.

Let's take a closer look at Cristina and the homework scenario. Cristina comes home from school, has a snack and is asked to do her homework. She completes everything in her backpack except math. Her mom asks her if there is anything else in her backpack for homework and she pulls out her math textbook. She stands up, textbook in hand, tosses it across the kitchen and shouts, "I hate math". Cristina then sits down and starts crying. This continues for an hour until dinner is ready. Cristina is asked to clear the table from her homework and set it for dinner. Cristina picks up her books, puts them in her backpack and she sets the table. She eats dinner with her family.

Looking at this a little more closely, the Antecedent is Mom asking if there is anything else in her backpack for homework. The behaviour is Cristina throwing the textbook across the room and shouting "I hate math," then sitting down and crying. The consequence is asking Cristina to clear the table from her homework and set it for dinner. Cristina's parents collect the data for several weeks. Each day the scenario is repeated. All of the homework is completed with the exception of math. Math homework is assigned daily, and it is in her backpack for the two weeks that the data is collected.

By examining the behavior and taking a closer look, one is able to determine the purpose behind her behavior. Is it for escape, attention, to receive something she wants or is there a sensory component to it? It allows us to hypothesize and determine a course of action that will enable us to help Cristina and change what is going on at the dinner table. In Cristina's case it took some digging to get to the bottom of things. It was clear, that the purpose behind the behavior was escape. Throw a tantrum, cry until dinner, get asked to put homework away, don't have to do math. But why? Cristina was a good student and had no problem completing any other homework. A phone call to the classroom teacher inquiring about Cristina's progress level in math ensued. It was revealed that Cristina had performed well on the first math test, which was a review of previous material learned, but had failed the next test. The work Cristina was assigned in math was hard and she continued to fall behind by not going back to where she first encountered a problem. A plan that would help Cristina was created and put into action. The classroom teacher offered extra help during the lunch hour and Cristina attended. She was able to start at the point just before she encountered a problem. Together she and her teacher worked, using manipulatives to demonstrate the concepts with lots of repetition and practice. Cristina caught up with her work, developed a rapport with her teacher, and was comfortable asking questions when she didn't understand something. Cristina performed well on her next test. Interestingly, the meltdowns during the after school homework time subsided. In fact, Cristina would often complete her homework in math first, meltdown free. Her mom would provide her with positive feedback.

There are so many ways to collect data, and for so many purposes. Educators collect data when testing students on their knowledge of a particular subject they have been studying. Companies graph the net profit and sales, and compare this to previous year performances. Stock value is graphed and compared over a period of time. And parents can collect data on their child's behavior and look for patterns. Data provides us with information, it can help us determine the purpose behind a behavior, and it can also provide accurate feedback.

In Cristina's case, data was collected to take a closer look at what was going on and to solve a problem she was having. It was a way to examine challenging behavior and the purpose behind it. The purpose behind Cristina's behavior was to escape or avoid completing her math homework. This was a clear cut example of behavior serving one purpose; to escape and avoid an undesirable activity. Sometimes behavior serves more than one purpose. It could serve as attention and escape. Regardless of the outcome, the collection of data provides feedback and informs, which in turn aids in decision making processes. It evaluates progress and assists in identifying skills that an individual needs to learn.

There are five steps that are required when collecting data. The first is to decide on what it is that you are collecting data on. Is it test performance, amount of time your child remains on task, or is it to identify the purpose behind a behavior and how it is serving your child? The second step is to identify the way in which data will be collected. Is it through an ABC chart, a count tally? Step three is determining who is collecting it. The fourth step is to record it. And finally, and most probably the most important step, is step five; to analyze it. The whole purpose of collecting the data is to learn if progress is being made and, if not, what can be done to change that.

Chapter 5

Under the Microscope – BULLYING

Jamie was always so eager to attend school. She would even get up early on the weekend and would often be found sitting at the kitchen table eating breakfast and looking out of the window for the school bus. School to Jamie was exciting and fun. Her face would light up with the mention of her teacher and friends. But things changed. Jamie's mom and dad noticed that Jamie stopped getting ready for school. She required many bedroom visits to make sure she was up, out of bed and getting dressed. Jamie began complaining about her stomach hurting and having a headache. Naturally her parents were very worried. The change seemed to occur over night. What was going on? Although Jamie had speech and was able to communicate her basic needs, she had challenges expressing how she felt. It was like prying teeth trying to get to the bottom of it. When questioned, Jamie would burst out into tears. She began to refuse to go to school. Jamie went from an excited, energetic and eager nine-year old to an isolated, withdrawn and anxious nine-year old who no longer smiled. Her parents took her to the doctor for a physical and Jamie received a clean bill of health. It wasn't until she was watching a television show that Jamie was able to communicate exactly what was bothering her. There was a scene about bullying. Jamie appeared very upset and indicated that she was very familiar with the scene. Finally, a clue! Jamie's mom and dad began piecing things together. They drew out characters to represent Jamie and the others. Jamie named them and wrote the words they said in speech bubbles. They then role- played what had happened. Now everyone had a clear picture of what had taken place. Jamie's parents met with the school administration and teachers to discuss next steps for Jamie. A bullying program was taught in the school and the students and teachers were taught what to do when bullying occurs.

Bullying is defined as unwanted or aggressive behavior. It has the potential to be repeated. There is a perceived or real imbalance of power between the perpetrator and the individual being bullied. Bullying can be verbal, social or physical. Verbal bullying is saying or writing hurtful things about an individual. Social bullying is hurting an individual's reputation or relationship with others. And physical bullying is causing harm to an individual or destroying their possessions. Bullying has no boundaries and can take place anywhere and affect anyone. It can happen in the workplace, the home, school and or community.

Cyberbullying includes being gossiped about, threatened, excluded from a group, or made to look bad online. Cyberbullying is bullying that involves an electronic device; a computer, a phone or tablet. It can be done through text messages, emails, social media sites, chat and websites. Cyberbullying can take place twenty-four hours per day, seven days per week. It can reach a large audience quickly, and once things are posted; they are difficult to remove. There is a printout available of the posts, emails, texts, fake profiles on websites or pictures and video. This provides evidence and makes the tracking down of the individual responsible relatively easy. However, the effects it has on the individual being targeted, as we have all seen, can be tragic. Individuals who have experienced cyberbullying often feel alone, in despair, isolated and lonely.

There may or may not be warning signs indicating that bullying is taking place. What is important as a parent is to be aware of changes in your child. A change in behavior such as eating and sleep patterns, physical ailments, a change in grades or not wanting to go to school are indicators to a parent that something is up. It does not necessarily mean that bullying is taking place. What it does indicate is that a closer look is required. Keeping the lines of communication open and asking how your child spent the lunch hour or recess can be conversation starters. Often children are reluctant to report things. This could be for a variety of reasons. As an individual being bullied, they may not feel confident in the school's ability to handle the situation. They may fear having to face the bully. If they are a bystander, they may fear becoming a target themselves. Perhaps the bully is a friend of theirs and they feel conflicted.

When your child has disclosed to you that they have experienced unwanted, mean or aggressive behavior either online or in person, the first thing to do is to reassure them that this is not their fault. Support them and discuss what happened. If the perpetrator is a friend of theirs, a conversation around what makes a good friend and some teaching in this area will be needed. Encourage your child to connect with other classmates. Teach him to stand up to his bully, to stay with his friends, and to always report when things happen. If the bullying is happening online, teach him not to respond. Commend him for being courageous and talking about it. Always keep the lines of communication between you and your child open, assuring him that he can come to you with anything.

If the bullying is taking place at school, the next step is to talk to the teacher and school principal. Avoid all temptations to address the issue yourself with the child or the parents of the child. It is important at the time of the meeting with the teacher and principal to discuss all that has been disclosed by your child; the words spoken or actions taken, the location, the time of day, the bystanders. There are many blind spots in school. Places such as the stairwell, change rooms, washrooms and on school buses are all locations where there may be less supervision. It is important to share this with the school. If a particular area is less supervised, changes can be implemented. Disclosing the time of day that the incidents occurred is also very important. Is it a time when classes are going on and stairwells and washrooms are generally unsupervised? Is it during entry or exit time? Is better supervision needed? As trivial as the information may appear, it is important to disclose all details; -- time, location, setting, and the event -- , verbatim.

Schools have policies in place and an investigation will need to occur. It is also important to ask for clarification as to how this situation will be handled. What is the policy, what steps will be taken, what are the procedures of the investigation and next steps, what type of education is going to be implemented or what programs are taught within the school to stop bullying? All of these questions are fair questions that administrators can answer.

Bullying affects the perpetrator, the individual being bullied, as well as the bystanders. Bullying is harmful and has lasting effects, sometimes fatal ones. Everyone has a right to feel safe, be treated with dignity, and respected. A bully needs to understand the effects their behavior has on others. An individual being bullied needs to understand positive relationships, and the bystander needs to understand that they are a part of this, and involving themselves brings change.

Developing trusting relationships between staff and students is a way to make students feel more comfortable about disclosing information. Trusting that the matters will be handled in a way that will not cause further harm to anyone is also paramount in the decision to disclose information, as both a bystander and an individual being bullied. Sometimes the bully is a popular individual who is fully immersed in the school community. This makes it even more challenging for an individual to report.

Promoting and building healthy relationships between staff and students can help. It will make an individual who is reporting an incident trust and know that the matter they are reporting will be taken seriously, with discretion and that they will be supported for being courageous and coming forward with something that is often very difficult. Some findings from research conducted by Dr. Wendy Craig of Queen's University and Dr. Debra Pepler of York University and the Hospital for Sick Children in Toronto demonstrate the power and effectiveness of bystanders intervening. Their observations revealed that when a bystander intervened, bullying stopped about half of the time within a 10 second time period.

Ultimately, it is the adults who are responsible for creating an environment that is nurturing and safe; one where positive, healthy relationships prevail. Our children are keen observers. They watch and do. Teaching them to be self-confident, to trust in their abilities, to lead, and to speak up and support each other are our responsibilities as parents, educators and members of community. As adults, it is also our responsibility to protect our children. This means to educate them about healthy relationships, and demonstrate what they are. As parents and educators we need to be aware of the social dynamics within social settings. Plan groups accordingly, pair individuals together who compliment and support one another. This can be done by looking at individual strengths. Similar individuals tend to gravitate towards one another; be aware of this and group individuals who have different strengths together.

Bullying is not a school problem, it is a community problem. It knows no boundaries and can happen virtually anywhere, from the hockey arena, to the dance recital, to the food court at the mall. As adults, when we witness it, we need to take action immediately. If there is something mean being said, we need to call it. Address it immediately before it goes any further. Praise and compliment positive interactions; interactions that are supportive, kind, and thoughtful. Build on a child's strengths and teach them the social skills they lack. This can be done through role-playing and acting out scenarios. Most importantly, if you see it or someone brings it to your attention, take immediate action. For more information visit www.prevnet.ca.

Chapter 6

Connor's Goosebumps on Steroids

Sensory overload, difficulty processing information, getting stuck, feeling overwhelmed – whatever you want to call it, individuals on the autism spectrum experience it. To someone looking from the outside in, and not through the lens of autism, it may not make sense. One individual on the autism spectrum described instrumental music class as "feeling like every violin is placed inside of my ear. I can't even see straight and I have no idea where I am." Another individual who usually has a pencil or a wrapper in his hand and is waving it in front of his face was asked why he did this. He said that this is the only way he can concentrate on his thoughts – by staring at the pencil or wrapper he holds in his hands.

Connor is an individual living with Asperger's syndrome. Asperger's syndrome is a form of autism. It is characterized by average or higher than average intellectual ability with deficits in the area of social skills. At the time of the interview he was eleven years of age. He takes us through an experience he has had.

Picture this: a gymnasium filled with one hundred and twenty grade six students. Tables along the peripheral of the room in the form of a U shape have papers taped to the edge with letters representing last names beginning with A all the way to Z. It is warm and the smells entering one's nostrils varies depending on where you are standing. You could catch the smell of stale cigarettes on clothing, the scent of Downy fabric softener, a whiff of Axe body spray, hairspray, or the stench of bad body odor. The visual is frightening: grade six students with their sleeves rolled up and adults injecting a needle into their upper arms. The height of the gymnasium ceiling amplifies the sound, the fans on the ceiling are spinning and the fluorescent lights are flickering. I am scared. The noise makes my head throb, like a heartbeat. It is Hepatitis B Immunization Day and I have been dreading it since I heard about it way back in September. My mom is here to support me but that isn't doing much good as I can't stop my brain from repeating thoughts of how painful needles are. My mom's logical words, "It will feel like a pinch" and "Just breathe" are being drowned by my own thoughts. Overpowered, her words and my thoughts become immersed in a whirlwind of confusion and overwhelm.

Connor: "When I am scared, it's like a thick heavy fog and I can't think straight. All that happens is the fear practically takes over. It's like I can't control my mouth but I can't control anything else either, especially when I am getting a needle or something. Last time I got a needle it wasn't too bad. This past Tuesday, we spent two hours just trying to get me in there and get through with the needle. I can still kinda feel it in my shoulder, actually if I really think about it ... that's one of the reasons I was so scared because I kept feeling like a deja vu in my shoulder of what the pain felt like, and that's what I kept imagining. Eventually I calmed down and got the shot. During the needle, my mom kept telling me to breathe and I was trying and then yelling, "This isn't working."

Mom: "It's like your brain knows it's just a little shot, but your body and your nerves can't listen to your brain. "

Connor: "My brain says, it's just a needle, it's okay. My body is 'AHHHH.' The only time my heart seems to increase speed is when I exercise. Usually you can feel your heart increase and I don't feel it so I don't think it increases when I am scared.

I went to the dentist and was supposed to get four teeth pulled out. Even with laughing gas and two needles, and numbing cream that pain just kept showing through. I still felt it. They started to pull a tooth out and I could still feel it. I was screaming until they stopped. Instead we are doing sleep dentistry but that might take a while to arrange."

Mom: "The anxiety Connor had at the dentist was overwhelming for him. He gave himself hives from anxiety. He was so nervous and scared and freaked out that his body actually reacted and he broke out in hives."

Connor: "So, it's like goosebumps on steroids. I use steroids a lot to describe stuff that is bigger than it normally is. When I am scared, my brain clouds up and the only thing I can see is fear. My head sees logic but when there is enough fear (in my brain this is what happens.) ... Usually if I have a distraction (that helps). A puppy calms me down. (Like)Whipper. (my dog)"

Connor's mom Lori describes one of the most challenging things is trying to get Connor to use the self-regulation strategies he knows, during a time when his goosebumps are on steroids.

Mom: "When my son gets frustrated there are usually arguments involved. Many frustrating things are about his rigidity and how he gets stuck with a certain idea or feeling and he can't let it go. In the past couple of weeks we have had a couple of extreme anxiety panic attack scenarios that revolved around medical issues. Shots where he gets so upset and freaked out and I feel helpless because there isn't anything that I can do. Even though I have strategies, he can't take them in at that moment, like he is able to when he is calm. But he can't actually take them in when he is anxious. That is incredibly frustrating, and I end up going around and around in circles and spending three hours on something that could have taken three minutes if it could have been communicated at a calm moment."

Connor: "When I am calm I have a better understanding of things. But if I am anxious it feels like there is a firewall between me and understanding. When I am really angry my eyes start to twitch and my muscles start to flex, and I think it is my head trying to scare off what is making me angry. Just naturally, my muscles seem to try and make myself look more intimidating."

Mom: "You start rocking and moving more. You also said to me that you have a thick heavy fog."

Connor: "No, that's when I am scared."

As a parent, providing our child with the basic needs -- a healthy diet and sufficient rest -- is an excellent start.

Maintaining secure and healthy relationships where our child feels supported and safe is also a requirement. But some kids need more. Self-regulation affects all areas of behavior; it affects our ability to concentrate, regulate our anger and frustration, regulate our thoughts, and get along with others. It affects us physically, socially, emotionally, and intellectually.

Dr. Stuart Shanker is Canada's leading expert in the area of self-regulation. He recommends four things that parents can do to improve a child's ability to self-regulate.

The first is to ensure that we are excellent detectives as parents. Know what our child's stressors are and what calms him down and keeps him alert. Keep a record of this and share it with your child's teacher and anyone else who spends time with him.

The second is exercise. The benefits of exercise are numerous. Provide an opportunity daily for this to take place. It could be going for a run together or engaging in any physical activity your child enjoys. Is it swimming, gymnastics, tennis, cycling, lifting, curling, or a hiking through a forest that is your child's preference? Whatever it is, embrace it and do it together.

The third is mindfulness programs. These programs can help your child identify where he is on a scale. Is he just right, too aroused or too low? Creating a system that is fun and one that your child identifies with can work. For example, if he has a favorite wind-up toy or character, use this to identify how his "self" feels. Let's think of a wind-up energizer bunny. When a wind-up toy is losing its stamina, it will slow down. Compare this to how he feels. Is he feeling too low and in need of some arousal? When the energizer bunny is fully wound up, he is doing back flips and is too aroused. Is this how he is feeling? And if so, what does he need to do to feel just right? When the energizer bunny is wound up just right, everything is running well. Is this how he feels? There are numerous visual supports out there that can assist your child in identifying his own self-arousal states. They come in the form of scales, charts, facial expressions, colors and words. The key is to find what works best for him.

The fourth is play. According to Dr. Stuart Shanker, when play emerges from a child's interest, it will engage his focus and encourage him to figure out what others are thinking; in other words, consider the perspective or others. The benefits of play are numerous.

Another key component in supporting your child is to be aware of your own emotions and regulate them closely. Do you find yourself feeling angry when your child is angry? Monitoring how you are feeling, what you are saying and how you are interacting with your child when he is having a challenging time self-regulating, is critical in having your child feel calm and alert.

Chapter 7

Behavior is Communication

You are feeling worried and stressed because your two-year old is not talking. Visits to the doctor indicate that his vision and hearing are within the normal ranges, but there is no speech. You have set up an appointment with a speech language pathologist as a next step. What can you do in the meantime? Take a closer look. Start by observing your child. How does he communicate his wants and needs? Is it through eye contact, reaching and pulling for the object, using a chair to get what he wants, or leading you by the hand? Whatever it is that he is doing, he is communicating his wants and needs through his behavior. What can you do now to help him? One way to encourage your child to communicate is to place a favorite toy of his in a container that is difficult to open. Give him the container making sure that the toy is visible to him and wait. The goal is to have him ask you for help opening the container. He may do this by passing you the container or gesturing for you to open it. As soon as he does, respond. Open the container, give him the toy and say, "Oh you want the _____." You could also model the phrase 'help please.' This will reinforce a socially acceptable way to communicate that help is needed. It is important that you respond in a consistent manner, accept all forms of communication and respond positively.

If you would like to teach your child how to sign for 'more' rather than to grab things, start with another person supporting this. The other person may have to model the gesture hand over hand. This means to physically place your hands on his and then gradually withdraw as he becomes more independent in gesturing for 'more'. One way to encourage this activity to continue to is use a highly motivating, high ticket item that your child wants. Perhaps it is a car rolling down a ramp or a container of bubbles. Begin by rolling the car down the ramp or blowing bubbles and then stop. Wait for a few moments and encourage him to ask for 'more' using the gesture. As soon as an attempt is made to ask for 'more,' continue with the activity. Remember to pair words with the action by saying, "You want more bubbles." The key to getting your child to request 'more' is to find highly motivating activities. It could be a favorite song; start it and then turn it off and wait. Perhaps it is tickles; tickle and then stop and wait. Maybe it is a favorite food. Always remember to reinforce the attempts made to communicate by communicating using specific and direct speech. Something like, "good job asking for more bubbles" is an example.

Offering your child a choice of two items is another way to encourage communication. Holding up the concrete objects and asking, "Do you want grapes or a banana?" and then waiting is a way to evaluate what his preference is, as well as the way he communicates. He may gaze at the item of preference, perhaps even reaching for it. Whatever he does, pair the action with the words, "I want a banana" or "I want grapes."

If he is successful making a choice with the concrete objects, you may want to try photographs of the items. Many individuals on the autism spectrum have strengths in visual processing and benefit greatly from visual supports. By building on this strength, we can increase independence and decrease our time talking and explaining. Visual supports are a constant; they remain, whereas speech is often lost or forgotten once it has been spoken. Our phones, shopping lists, agenda and to do lists are everyday examples of the visual supports we use regularly. A visual support or an image often clarifies meaning and brings words to life. If I were to say the word 'bridge' one might not understand it until I paired it with a picture. Pictures give us a clear image of the message one is trying to convey. Pictures speak a universal language.

Play is another way to encourage communication between you and your child. Choose toys that your child likes, and ones that can teach a variety of skills. Think about categories and examples from each one. Some examples of categories are body parts, food, and clothing. Reinforce the vocabulary while engaging in play. Perhaps you are using a magnetic puzzle or play dough and making a character's face. Words that can be reinforced are eyes, nose, mouth, ears and hair. Perhaps you are playing a dress-up game or you are dressing up a puppet or a doll. Label the articles of clothing. Maybe you are playing with velcro fruit or food puzzles. Once your child has been exposed to a category through play, you can see whether or not he understands the vocabulary receptively by playing a game. Place the articles on a table or an area where he is comfortable. Ask him to give you the apple or the banana. Focus on one category at a time. When teaching your child vocabulary through play, you want to remember to ensure that you have his attention before speaking. Speak clearly using a single word or short phrases. Pair each word with the object or picture and get down to his level; kneel down or sit to get to his eye level. Remember to allow time for a response. It can take your child longer to respond for many reasons.

Imitation is the ability to copy. And the ability to imitate is a critical component in the development of a child. You can teach your child basic imitation skills through repetition. Keep it simple by starting with a motor activity. Try a pot and two spoons. Sit across from him, ensure you have his attention and begin banging the spoon on the pot. Encourage him to copy. If there is no response, support him by placing your hand on top of his and bang the spoon on the pot. Gradually reduce the level of support and see if he imitates your action of banging the spoon on the pot. If he does not, provide him with the support he needs.

Imitation can be done with vocalizations as well. If your child vocalizes spontaneously, imitate the sound he has just made and wait and see if he responds by making the same sound again. If he does, continue the 'conversation' and let him know how thrilled you are. Take this a step further by starting a new sound and encouraging him to imitate. See if it continues and if so, continue expanding and building. If he does not continue, make the same sound a few times, to see if he continues. Building on this and taking it to the next step could be teaching him how to imitate the sound of objects. For example, a clock says 'tick tock' and a train 'choo choo.' A car can say 'beep beep' and a bell 'ding dong.'

Teaching your child to imitate another person's actions can begin with something as simple as waving bye or clapping hands. If you are teaching your child how to clap his hands, sit across from him, gain his attention and begin clapping your hands. If your child is unsure of what to do, take his hands and clap them. Continue to provide him with some level of support, gradually reducing it with each interaction. Let your child know that he is doing well by providing him with positive feedback after each appropriate response. As your child becomes more successful, this activity can be paired with music; perhaps a favorite song that incorporates actions.

Turn-taking is another way to encourage reciprocal interactions. This can be done through a structured game or a physical activity. Some examples are jumping on a trampoline, sitting on a teeter totter, or rolling a ball back and forth. Whatever the activity is, it is important to be animated, and the activity fast-paced to capture and sustain his attention. Encourage him to request more. Do this by stopping and waiting. He may indicate that he wants more by looking, vocalizing, signing for 'more,' moving his body or gesturing. Accept all of them and respond in a positive animated manner by saying something like, 'good asking, you want more!'

To encourage your child to request engaging in play, engage in a fun activity with another person; another child if possible. Be animated and excited about the activity. See if your child indicates or signals that he is interested in joining. Remember to choose an activity that is highly motivating to your child.

Continue to encourage play. Explore new toys and play activities. Be a keen observer and see what new toys he gravitates towards. Explore imaginative or symbolic play by playing in a house center, talking on the phone or having a tea party.

Use what motivates and interests your child. Have a system in place and use it in every environment. If you are working with a speech language pathologist, implement their suggestions at home. Share the information with the daycare, babysitter or school he attends. Set up a meeting to share information about your child with all of his caregivers. If your child is using a form of communication in one environment, use it across all environments and ensure that whatever materials he needs with him in order for this to happen, come with him always.

Chapter 8

Navigating the Social World

As parents we want what is best for our children. A parent wants their children to be successful. This can mean a different thing for each of us as parents. It could be a want or desire for your child is to have a meaningful relationship with the significant people in their lives. It could be a desire for your child to be functioning independently and contributing to their purpose as an adult. Success can mean different things for different people, and it can also change at different stages in your child's life.

As a baby and toddler, the formative years are spent developing a secure and healthy relationship with you as a parent, a caregiver and family. As a child grows into preteen years, it is a time for your child to have a set of core friends who are supportive and fun to be with. When your child enters the teenage years, a lot of things take place. Puberty sets in, and your child physically changes into a young man or young woman. Sometimes their friends change or their friends' interests change. Regardless of the stage your child is in, having well- developed social skills will enable him to transition into these different stages with ease. Individuals on the autism spectrum do not learn social skills through observation alone. An individual on the autism spectrum requires direct instruction and opportunities for repeated practice in a variety of different settings. Starting early is one of the best things you can do for your child.

In order to know how you can help your child best, you need to be a keen observer. Different strategies will work, depending on your child's age and where he is at this particular stage in his life. Understanding that connecting with another individual requires taking the perspective of another person is sometimes hard for neurotypicals. Connecting, is seeing how another person views the world. This ability does not come naturally to an individual on the autism spectrum and needs to be taught explicitly.

While in different settings, observe how your child acts. Does he sit in a sandbox in the park next to others or does he prefer to sit alone? Is he aware of other children around him? Does he respond to his name? By gathering this information, a plan can be put into place. Depending on how he responds, a turn taking play activity could begin with another child in the sandbox, or with you. Take turns shoveling sand into the bucket. But remember, this is tough work for him, and he may want to do his own thing, so end the play on a positive note. If it lasts 30 seconds, aim for 35 seconds next time.

Perhaps you have noticed that whenever your child is playing alongside others at a park and sees a toy he wants, he grabs it out of another child's hand rather than asking for it. You have noticed that this happens in a variety of environments with a variety of people. Creating a book with photos and a sentence or two beneath the pictures is one way to teach him how to ask for something, rather than grabbing it. Unlike words, the book is a constant 'go to' item that serves as a teaching tool.

Jane and I are sitting in the sandbox. She has a red shovel and I have a blue one. I want the red shovel because red is my favorite color. I can look at her, until she looks at me, and ask her if we can trade shovels. I will wait for her answer. Asking a friend for a toy is the right way to do things. Jane may say yes; , she may say no, or she may say maybe later. Either way, I accept her answer and continue with what I am doing or find something else to play with.

Perhaps your child greets everyone with a hug, no matter who they are. Although this may seem cute now at a young age, fast forward ten years and notice how people's perceptions of things change quickly. That is why it is important to teach your child the different ways to greet someone, depending on who they are now. This can be done through personalized stories that are created to describe each individual family makeup. Photos of members of your family and 'inner circle' persons can be taken and a sentence or two written beneath the picture. These could be printed off and bound together. That way there is a reference that visually represents what you are trying to teach. Other members in the community could be added into the book with a description of how to greet each person. For example, a bus driver can be greeted by saying good morning and smiling. These skills will need to be taught in a variety of different environments, with a variety of people, to ensure he understands.

Understanding what another person is thinking and feeling is a critical component of understanding how to respond in a given situation and what to do. Teaching your child this can be done while reading a story together, or watching a show together and discussing it. While reading a story, ask him what he thinks a particular character feels. Ask him how the character's face looks when feeling that way. Have him draw it out or show you. Continue this exercise until he is able to identify how others are feeling and read facial expressions.

As your child grows, so do the number of environments and social setting he may find himself in. His social world expands and he will have to learn how to navigate it. High school, part- time job, friends, dating, job interviews, college, living away from home, working and living with others are all considerations. Let's begin with high school. It is a very different environment and the expectations, both academically and socially, change. Friends begin to date; your child may be interested in dating someone, but doesn't know how to approach it. Finding your child a support group in your community for teens with autism can help him. It would provide a safe environment for him to discuss these concerns around dating, as well as an opportunity to meet individuals who may be going through the same thing.

Teaching your child how to express his likes, dislikes, and obstacles he encounters openly and appropriately at an early age will help. Teaching him that there is always a solution to a problem will also allow him to face his fears. Starting something new and doing something different can make many, not just individuals with autism, feel fearful. This is because it means stepping out of your comfort zone. Do it anyway. Recognize the fear, confront it, talk about it and do it. Visualization techniques work for many. Having your child visualize that the fear is like a vapor, may help him in containing the fear and making it disappear.

Navigating the social world and understanding what others are saying through their word choices as well as their body language requires practice. Role-playing different actions and scenarios is a way to teach your child what different actions mean. For example, ask him how a person demonstrates that they are bored, excited, or nervous about something. Watching a television series together about high school can generate some excellent conversation starters, as well as valuable lessons.

If your child is going for a job interview he can prepare in many ways. First, knowing what to wear to that interview, how to greet the person interviewing, how to sit with the correct posture and answer the questions, where to look when asked a question are all things that coaches, parents, teachers and supportive friends can assist with. Repeated practice in a variety of different settings with different people will be beneficial.

Moving away from home for the very first time can be overwhelming. Managing one's time, being responsible for money management, shopping, meal preparation, laundry, housekeeping and producing either at school or work can seem daunting. But there are many things that can be done in order to prepare your child for this. Start early, by teaching your child how to do laundry and having him do his own laundry weekly at home. This can be a part of an allowance program. Having your child help with the meal preparation at home can also ensure independence. This can be a gradual transition. Teach him to cook with you and then transition to more independence by having him preparing a simple meal a few times a week. If done gradually over time, the feeling of overwhelm will not be so great. Teaching your child how to creating a shopping list or, a weekly menu, and how to do housework are all skills that can be taught at an early age and will teach independence. Teach him how to dust, vacuum, wash dishes, iron clothes, put things away and generally maintain a clean, organized environment. One functions and works more productively in an environment like this. All of these are goals, that we as parents need to plan for, with our child in mind. Ask, what do I need to do to have my child function as independently as possible as a young adult? Begin with an end in mind. Is the goal to have him living independently? If so, then what steps do I need to teach him and take in order to ensure that this is the outcome? It is thinking backwards and planning forwards.

Chapter 9

Mental Health Hygiene

Maintaining healthy habits makes sense, but when one has too many things going on, or we are spread too thinly, healthy habits are usually the first things to go. Perhaps the regular workout may be skipped, or the meals that you would usually prepare on a Sunday afternoon are replaced with takeout meals during a busy week. Think about the holiday season or a busy time at work. Did you experience too many late nights? Perhaps an overdose of sugar?

The three components of health hygiene are nutrition, sleep and exercise. When any of these components are missing from our routine, we feel it and so do those around us. It may be the person who serves you your regular coffee at Starbucks, maybe it's the person who cuts you off while driving, maybe it's your significant other, or your child with whom you are short, or bad-tempered, or reactive with. Eating right, exercising and sleeping adequately are necessary for us to be operating at an optimum level. And when we are operating at an optimum level, we are prepared to handle whatever we need to handle. It could be a temper tantrum, a refusal to go to bed, a squabble amongst siblings, a dishwasher that has broken, a flood, or a loss of employment. Whatever it may be, we are better able when we practice the three components of health hygiene. As a parent, it is important to ensure that our child also practices health hygiene.

There are many other practices we can incorporate into our lives and the lives of our children which are extremely beneficial. One of them is deep breathing. Breathing in for four counts and as you are breathing in expand your belly – imagine how a balloon expands. Hold your breath for four counts and then exhale for four counts. It is one of the simplest things to practice, once learned and one of the most effective. It not only brings oxygen to all of the organs and slows our heart rate, but it allows us to be present and aware of our breath. Consider it a time to check in and assure yourself that everything is okay. Teaching your child to deep breathe may take some time. A good place to start is by having them learn to blow. Blow a whistle, a paper windmill, or some tissue paper across the table. Continue to practice this, building up to the goal of having them breathing in and out slowly. Having them place a hand on their belly and feel the air expand and contract is another option.

Meditation has been around for centuries, and there are many options available. One common practice used in many schools today is a guided meditation. A quiet location and a comfortable position are two requirements. Start by closing your eyes, dimming the lights, sitting or lying down in a comfortable position and listening to the words spoken. It takes practice to lay still. Some find themselves overwhelmed with thoughts. That's okay; accept them and let them go. Some may fall asleep. Whatever happens, it is okay. There is no right or wrong way to meditate. The key is to do it frequently; daily for ten minutes would be ideal. The comments from students and individuals participating in this is that they look forward to this practice, and ask their teacher if it is possible to start every class with a guided meditation. Many teachers have reported how beneficial it is for their students and themselves. It works; try it.

Teaching your child that they are responsible for their behavior is important. Some tools to teach this are thermometer scales or behavior scales that you can create to suite your child's or your own needs. Sometimes, entire families use a scale to let other members know where they are and how they are feeling. For simplicity purposes, a scale from one to five or one to three could be used. As the numbers increase on the scale, so does the intensity of the behavior. For example, a five on the scale means I am ready to explode, or I am going to lose it, whereas a one represents I am calm and in a good place. A two on the scale could mean I am a little worried about .... A three on the scale would indicate that a person is feeling anxious or upset about something, and so on. A scale of one to three has been used as colors on a traffic light. Green or number one means, I am good to go. Two or yellow means, I need to do something to change where I am and calm down. And three means, I am out of control or in the red and I need to stop. There are so many variations of this, and the scales are meant to be created and implemented according to an individual's needs. It is a way to self-monitor as well as to truly know one's self.

Visualization is a tool used by many athletes. It is a way to imagine successfully completing something that you find stressful in a successful way. So a sprinter would visualize herself completing the race in top form and best time. Visualizing herself winning the race, and going through the process is helpful for many athletes. Creating a mental image of what one wants to happen, improves one's self-confidence and belief in one's ability. For example, if your child becomes anxious before writing a test, have him visualize himself studying and understanding the notes. Have him visualize himself writing the test and understanding all of the content. Try it on yourself. Think of something that you are worried about. Visualize yourself going through the stressful event successfully. Include all of your senses; how your body feels, the sounds you hear, the smell, what you see. Imagine it as vividly as you can. If you are unable to get a picture or an image of an upcoming stressful event, but feel anxious, think of a happy place. It could be an image of a beach, a forest, a place you have visited, or an activity that you enjoy. Repeat phrases such as; I am relaxed, I am at ease, tension is being released out of my body, I feel at peace. Try this two to three times per day.

We are bombarded with thousands of thoughts daily, many of them unnecessary and unpleasant. Step number one is to be aware of your thoughts and words. Negative thoughts breed negative thoughts. Positive thoughts bring about positive feelings. The power of positive thinking and remembering that we are in control of our thoughts is a process. This takes some inner work. We can truly change the way we feel by changing the way we think. Many of our thoughts and beliefs have been developed as young children. The environment we grew up in, the words we heard spoken, the thoughts of others influence and affect us. Listening to our words, and developing an awareness of our thoughts, and changing the negative ones into positive ones, can impact ourselves and all who are a part of our lives. It also impacts our children.

Yoga is also a practice that has been around for years. The benefits are many; improved posture and flexibility, increased muscle tone, and overall well-being. It is a practice that places a lot of emphasis on breath, and breathing deeply and rhythmically through the belly. The focus is on being present and on your mat, and leaving the outside world out there away from the practice. It is becoming increasingly popular in schools and with children.

Cognitive behavior therapy is a common type of mental health counseling. It is performed by a mental health therapist and is an effective tool in helping an individual dealing with a stressful situation. It would be best to consult with a physician for more information.

Exploring and knowing oneself will provide one with a better understanding of self. Ask yourself "what is it that calms me and my child down after a particularly stressful event?" Is it a listening to music, going for a run, swinging on a swing set or tire, watching a movie? Knowing these things aids in the self-regulation process and are critical in going from a 5 to a 1 without incident. Identifying activities that calm oneself down and taking the necessary actions and steps will get your child to a one in the quickest amount of time possible.

There are many mental health hygiene methods mentioned in this chapter. What is most important is that you find one that works for you and your child. The benefits of health hygiene are numerous and affect every aspect of our lives.

Notes

Notes

Notes